# FISHER'S CAPITAL
# AND INCOME

## BY

## THORSTEIN B. VEBLEN

**British Library Cataloguing-in-Publication Data**
A catalogue record for this book is available from the
British Library

# Contents

# Thorstein Veblen

Thorstein Bunde Veblen was born Torsten Bunde Veblen on 30th July 1857 in Cato, Wisconsin, United States, to Norwegian immigrant parents.

Veblen grew up on his parents farm in Nerstrand, Minnesota. This area and others like it were known as little Norways due to the religious and cultural traditions that had been imported from the old country. Although Norwegian was his first language, the young Veblen learned English from neighbours and at school.

His parents put a lot of emphasis on education and hard work and at age seventeen he was sent to study at Carleton College Academy. It was there that he met John Bates Clark (1847–1938) who went on to become a leader in the new field of neoclassical economics. Upon graduating Veblen conducted graduate work under Charles Sanders Pierce (the founder of the pragmatist school in philosophy) at John Hopkins University. He then moved to Yale in 1884 to take a Ph.D. and completed his dissertation on "Ethical Grounds of a Doctrine of Retribution."

Upon leaving Yale he was unable to find a employment. This was partly due to prejudice against Norwegians, and partly because most universities considered him insufficiently educated in Christianity; most academics at the time held divinity degrees. Due to this, Veblen returned to the family farm – ostensibly to recover from malaria – and spent six years there reading voraciously. However, in 1891 he was accepted to study economics as a graduate student at Cornell University. From here on his academic career took off, obtaining his first professional appointment at the University of Chicago – where in 1900 he was promoted to assistant professor – and from there moving on work at institutions including Stanford University and the University of Missouri.

Veblen drew from the work of 19th century intellectuals such as Charles Darwin and Herbert Spencer to develop a 20th century theory of evolutionary economics. He described economic behaviour as socially determined and saw economic organization as a process of ongoing evolution. In his work *The Theory of the Leisure Class* (1899) he outlined how rich and poor alike, attempt to impress others and seek to gain advantage through what Veblen coined "conspicuous consumption" and the ability to engage in "conspicuous leisure." In *The Theory of Business Enterprise* (1904) he used evolutionary analysis to explain the growth of business combinations and trusts.

In the 21st century his ideas have come back into the spotlight as a valid approach for studying the intricacies of economic systems and his theory that humans do not rationally pursue value and utility is one of the cornerstones of the modern discipline of behavioural economics. Veblen made a lasting contribution to his field and has influenced many scholars that have followed him.

Thorstein Veblen died in California on 3rd August 1929, less than three months before the crash of the U.S. Stock market crash which led to the great depression.

# FISHER'S CAPITAL AND INCOME

Political Science Quarterly, Volume 23, (1908)

The Nature of Capital and Income(1*) is of that class of books that have kept the guild of theoretical economists content to do nothing toward "the increase and diffusion of knowledge" during the past quarter of a century. Of this class Mr Fisher's work is of the best -- thoughtful, painstaking, sagacious, exhaustive, lucid, and tenaciously logical. What it lacks is the breath of life; and this lack it shares with the many theoretical productions of the Austrian diversion as well as of the economists of more strictly classical antecedents. Not that Mr Fisher's work falls short of the mark set by those many able men who have preceded him in this field. No reader of Mr Fisher can justly feel disappointed in his performance of the difficult task which he sets himself. The work performs what it promises and does it in compliance with all the rules of the craft. But it does not set out substantially to extend the theory or to contribute to the sum of knowledge, either by bringing hitherto refractory phenomena into the organised structure of the science, or by affording farther or more comprehensive insight into the already familiar processes of modern economic life. Consistently with its aim, it is a work of taxonomy, of definition and classification; and it is carried through wholly within the limits imposed by this its taxonomic aim. There are many shrewd observations on the phenomena of current business, and much evidence of an extensive and intimate acquaintance with such facts of modern culture as are still awaiting scientific treatment at the hands of the economists (e.g., in chapters v and vi, "Capital Accounts" and "Capital Summation", as also in chapters viii, ix, xiii, xiv, "Income Accounts", "Income Summation", "Value of Capital", "Earnings and Income", "The Risk Element"). But the facts of observation so drawn into the discussion are chiefly drawn in to illustrate or fortify an argument, somewhat polemical, not as material calling for theoretical explanation. As affects the development of the theory, these observations and this information run along on the side and are not allowed to disturb the argument in its secure march toward its taxonomic goal.

There is no intention here to decry taxonomy, of course. Definition and classification are as much needed in economics as they are in those other sciences which have already left the exclusively taxonomic standpoint behind. The point of criticism, on this head, is that this class of economic theory differs from the modern sciences in being substantially nothing but definition and classification. Taxonomy for taxonomy's sake, definition and classification for the sake of definition and classification, meets no need of modern science. Work of this class has no value and no claims to consideration except so far as it is of use to the science in its endeavor to know and explain the processes of life. This test of usefulness applies even more broadly in economics and similar sciences of human conduct than in the natural sciences, commonly so-called. It is on this head, as regards the serviceability of his taxonomic results, that Mr Fisher's work falls short. A modern science has to do with the facts as they come to hand, not with putative phenomena warily led out from a primordial metaphysical postulate, such as the "hedonic principle". To meet the needs of science, therefore, such modern concepts as "capital" and "income" must be defined by observation rather than by ratiocination. Observation will not yield such a hard-and-fast definition of the term as is sought by Mr Fisher and his co-disputants, a definition which shall mark off a pecuniary concept by physical distinctions, which shall be good for all times and places and all economic situations, ancient and modern, whether there is investment of capital or not.

"Capital" is a concept much employed by modern men of affairs. If it were not for the use of the concept in economic affairs -- its growing use for a century past -- the science would not be concerned about the meaning of the term today. It is this use of the concept in the conduct of affairs that obtrudes it upon the attention of economists; and it is, primarily at least, for a better knowledge of these pecuniary affairs, in which the concept of capital plays so large a part, that a better knowledge of the concept itself is sought. As it plays its part in these affairs of business, the concept of capital is, substantially, a habit of thought of the men engaged in business, more or less closely defined in practice by the consensus of usage in the business community. A serviceable definition of it therefore, for the use of modern science, can be got only by observation of the current habits of thought of business men. This painfully longwinded declaration of what must appear to be a patent truism so soon as it is put in words may seem a gratuitous insistence on a stale commonplace. But it is an even more painfully tedious fact that the current polemics about "the capital concept" goes on year after year without recognition of this patent truism.

What may help to cover, rather than to excuse, the failure of many economists to resort to observation for a knowledge of what the term "capital" means is the fact, adverted to by the way in various writers, that business usage of the term is not uniform and stable; it does not remain the same from generation to generation; and it cannot, at least as regards present usage, be identified and defined by physical marks. The specific marks of the concept -- the characteristics of the category -- in the common usage are not physical marks, and the categories with which it is, in usage, related and contrasted are not categories that admit of definition in material terms; because it is, in usage, a pecuniary concept and stands in pecuniary relations and contrasts with other categories. It is a pecuniary term, primarily a term of investment, and as such, as a habit of thought of the men who have to do with pecuniary affairs, it necessarily changes in response to the changes going forward in the pecuniary situation and in the methods of conducting pecuniary affairs. "Capital", is the usage of current business, undoubtedly has not precisely the same meaning as it had in the corresponding usage of half a century ago; and it is safe to say that it will not retain its present meaning, unimpaired and unimproved, in the usage of ten years hence; nor does it cover just the same details in one connection as in another. Yet business men know what the term means to them. With all its shifting ambiguities, they know it securely enough for their use. The concept has sufficient stability and precision to serve their needs; and, if the economist is to deal with the phenomena of modern life in which this concept serves a use of first-rate importance, he must take the term and the concept as he finds them. It is idle fatigue to endeavor to normalise them into a formula which may suit his prepossessions but which is not true to life. The mountain will not come to Mahomet.

It is not for its idiosyncrasies that Mr Fisher's analysis and formulation of the "capital concept" merits particular attention, but because it is the most elaborate outcome of classificatory economics to this date. Except for certain minor features -- important, no doubt, within the school

-- his definition of capital is by no means a wide departure. It is only worked out more consistently, painstakingly, and circumspectly than has hitherto been done. Some of these special features peculiar to Mr Fisher's position have been carefully and very ably discussed by Mr Fetter.(2*) The merits of the discussion of these matters between the critic and his author, with the incidental balancing of accounts, need not detain the present argument. Nor need particular attention here be given to the points in dispute so far as regards their consistency with the general body of theory upheld by Mr Fisher and other economists who cultivate the classificatory science. But there are some details of the "nature of capital" as set forth by Mr Fisher -- and in large part assented to by Mr Fetter and others of the life way of thinking -- that require particular attention as regards their adequacy for other purposes than that of a science of classification.

(1) In the general definition of "capital" (e.g., pp. 51-53, 66-68, 324), the concept is made to comprise all wealth (in its relation to future income); and "wealth" has, in the same as well as in earlier pages, been defined "to signify material objects owned by human beings," which, in turn, includes all persons, as well as other material objects. As an aggregate, therefore, as an outcome of a comprehensive "capital summation," "capital" comprises the material universe in so far as the material universe may be turned to use by man (see p. 328). This general definition includes too much and

too little. A serviceable definition of capital, one that shall answer to the concept as it is found in practice in the habits of thought of business men, will not include persons. Hitherto, there is no question, the distinction between the capitalist and his capital is not disregarded by practical men, except possibly by way of an occasional affectation of speech; and it is highly improbable that, at any point in the calculable future, business men can come habitually to confuse these two disparate concepts. Modern business proceeds on the distinction. It is only in pulpit oratory that a man's person is legitimately spoken of as an item of his assets. And as for a business man's capitalising other persons, the law does not allow it, even in the form of peonage. There are also other material objects "under the dominion of man" which are not currently thought of as items of capital.

There are apparently two many perplexities of the mechanical classification which constrain Mr Fisher to include the person of the owner among the owner's assets as capital: (a) Contrary to business usage, he is required by his premises to exclude immaterial wealth because it is not amenable to classification by mechanical tests, and it is therefore necessary to find some roundabout line of approach to such elements as good will, and the like;(3*) and (b) persons are conceived to yield income (in the sense of Mr Fisher's definition of "income" presently to be noted), and since capital is held to be anything which yields "income"

-- indeed "capital" is such by virtue of its yielding "income" -- persons are included under "capital" by force of logic, though contrary to fact.

(2) As has already been indicated in passing, "immaterial wealth", or "intangible assets", is excluded from "capital" in Mr Fisher's analysis. Indeed, the existence of intangible assets is denied. The phrase is held to be an untoward misnomer for certain classes of property rights in material objects which are not wholly owned by the individual to whom these property rights inure. An important part of these incomplete property rights are rights of quasi-ownership in other persons, or claims to services performed by such persons. This denial of immaterial wealth Mr Fisher intends as a salutary correction of current business usage (see p. 39); and he takes pains to show how, by a cumbersome ratiocination (see chapter ii, sections 6-10), the term "intangible assets" may be avoided without landing the theory in the instant confusion which a simple denial of the concept would bring about. As a correction of current usage the attempted exclusion of intangible assets from "capital" does not seem a wise innovation. It cripples the definition for the purposes which alone would make a definition worth while. The concept of intangible assets is present in current usage on no such doubtful or precarious tenure as could be canceled by a bit of good advice. Its vogue is growing and its use is becoming more secure and more definite. The habit and the necessity

of taking account, under one name or another, of the various immaterial items of wealth classed as intangible assets counts for more and more in the conduct of affairs; and any theory that aims to deal with the actualities of modern business will have to make its peace with the term or terms by which these elements of capital are called, however wrong-headed a habit it may be conceived to be. The men of affairs find the concept serviceable, or rather they find it forced upon them, and the theorist of affairs cannot afford to dispense with a concept which is so large a constituent in the substance of affairs.

But the fault of the definition at this point is more serious than the mere exclusion of a serviceable general term which might be avoided by a circumlocution. "Intangible assets" is not simply a convenient general term covering certain more or less fluctuating property rights in certain material items of wealth. The elements of capital so designated are chiefly of the nature of differential advantages of a given business man, or a given concern, as against another. But they are capitalised in the same way as tangible items of wealth are capitalised, and in large part they are covered by negotiable securities, indistinguishable, and in most cases inseparable from, securities representing tangible assets. So, being blended in the process of capitalisation with the tangible assets, the securities based on the intangible assets create claims of ownership co-ordinate with those based on the material items and enter, in practice, into "capital summation" on the same footing as other items of wealth. Hence they become a basis of credit extensions, serving to increase the aggregate claims of creditors beyond what the hypothecable material wealth of the debtors would satisfy. Hence, in a period of general liquidation, when the differential advantages of the various concerns greatly contract, the legitimate claims of creditors come greatly to exceed the paying capacity of debtors, and the collapse of the credit system follows. The failure of classical theory to give an intelligent account of credit and crises is in great part due to the habitual refusal of economists to recognise intangible assets, and Mr Fisher's argument is, in effect, an accentuation of this ancient infirmity of the classical theory.

It may be added that differential competitive advantages cannot be added together to make an aggregate even apart from the tangible items of "capital wealth", since the advantage of one concern is the disadvantage of another. These assets come forth, grow great, and decay, according to the advance or decline of the strategic advantage achieved by given individuals or business concerns. Their "summation" is a spurious summation, in the main, since they represent competitive advantages, in the main; and their capitalisation adds a spurious volume to the aggregate property rights of the community. So that it follows from the capitalisation of these items of differential wealth, particularly when they are covered by vendible securities, that the aggregate property rights of the community come to exceed the aggregate wealth of the community.(4*) This is, of course, a sufficiently grave trait of the modern business situation, but the effect of Mr Fisher's contention is to deny its existence by the turn of a phrase and to put economic theory back where it stood before the modern situation had arisen. There are other turns in modern business affairs traceable to the vogue of this concept of "intangible assets," but this illustration of its grave consequences should be a sufficient caution to any taxonomist who endeavors to simplify his scheme of definition by denying inconvenient facts.

The point is perhaps sufficiently plain from what has been said, but it will bear specific mention that the apparent success of Mr Fisher's analysis of intangible assets (pp. 32-40, 96-97) is due to his not going beyond the first move. So soon as the actualities of business complication and the cumulative effects of capitalisation are taken into account, it is evident that, with the best intentions, Mr Fisher's explanation of intangible assets as a roundabout claim to certain concrete (tangible) items of wealth will not serve. The treatment of credit suffers from a like unwillingness to accept the facts of observation or to look farther than the first move in an analysis. This shortsightedness of the taxonomic economist is a logical consequence of the hedonistic postulates of the school, not a personal peculiarity of the present or any other author.

As to Mr Fisher's definition and handling of the second concept with which the book is occupied -- income -- much the same is true as of the discussion of capital. Income is re-defined with a close adherence to the logic of that hedonistic-taxonomic system of theory for which he speaks. The concept of income here offered is more tenaciously consistent with the logical run of current classificatory economics, perhaps, than any that has been offered before. It is the perfect flower of economic taxonomy, and it shows, as no previous exposition of the kind has shown, the inherent futility of this class of work for other than purely taxonomic ends.

The concept of income, like that of capital, is well at home in current business usage; and professedly, it is the concept of income as it plays its part in the affairs of business that occupies the author's attention. But here, again, as before, the definition -- "the nature of income" -- is not worked out from observation of current facts, with an endeavor to make the demarcation of the concept square with the habitual apprehension of the phenomena of income in the business community. Taken at its current import, as the concept is taken in the run of business and in the economic affair of any community of men dominated by the animus of business enterprise, there can be no question but that "income" is a pecuniary concept; it is money income, or is as an element which is convertible into terms of money income and amenable to the pecuniary scheme of accountancy. As a business proposition, nothing that cannot be rated in terms of money income is to be accounted income at all; which is the same as saying that no definition which goes beyond or behind the pecuniary concept can be a serviceable definition of income for modern use. There may be something beyond or behind this pecuniary concept which it may be desirable to reach and discuss for some other purpose more or less germane to the affairs of modern life; but such a something, whatever its nature, cannot be called "income" in the same sense in which that term is employed in modern business usage. When the term is applied to such an extra-pecuniary or praetor-pecuniary concept, such as an extension of the term is a rhetorical license; it is a figure of speech which is bound to work confusion in any argument or analysis that deals with the two inconvertible concepts. "Income" in modern usage, is a business concept; "psychic income" is not; and, as Mr Fisher is in an eminently good position to admit, the two are incommensurable, or rather disparate, magnitudes. The one cannot be reduced to terms of the other. This state of the case may be deprecated, but it cannot be denied; and it is no service to the science of modern economic life to confuse this distinction by running the two under one technical term.

Chapter xiv ("Earnings and Income"), and more particularly the latter sections of the chapter, illustrate how far from facts one may be led by a consistent adherence to Mr Fisher's hedonistic working-out of the concept of income. "To regard 'savings' as income is essentially to regard an increase of capital as income" (pp. 254-253). Now, apart from the hedonistic prepossession, there is, of course, no reason for not regarding such an increase of capital as income. The two ideas -- "income" and "increase of capital" -- are by no means mutually exclusive in the current usage; and ordinarily, so long as the terms are taken in their current (pecuniary) meaning, such an increase of capital would unhesitatingly be rated as income to the owner. The need of making "income" and "increase of capital" mutually exclusive categories is a need incident to a mechanically drawn scheme of classification, and it disappears so soon as classification for classification's sake is given up. It is traceable to a postulated (hedonistic) principle presumed to rule men and things, not to observation of the run of facts in modern life. Indeed, even in Mr Fisher's analysis the distinction goes into abeyance for a while where, in the doctrine of "capital value" (chapter xiii, especially section 11, and chapter xvlii, section 2) the facts will absolutely not tolerate its being kept up. The hedondistic taxonomy breaks down at this juncture. And the fact is significant that this point of doctrine -- viz., that capital considered as a magnitude of value "is the discounted value of the expected income" -- is the latest and most highly prized advance in economic theory to whose initiation Mr Fisher's writings give him a defensible claim. (5*)

The day when Bentham's conception of economic life was serviceable for the purposes of contemporary science lies about one hundred years back, and Mr Fisher's reduction of "income" to "psychic income" is late by that much. The absolute merits of the hedonistic conception of economic theory need not be argued here. It was a far-reaching conception, and its length of life has made it a grand conception. But great as may be the due of courtesy to that conception for the long season of placid content which economic theory has spent beneath its spreading chestnut tree, yet the fact is not to be overlooked that is scheme of accountancy is not that of the modern business community. The logic of economic life in a modern community runs in terms of pecuniary, not of hedonistic magnitudes.

Mr Fisher's farthest advance, his definition and handling of "capital value" involves the breaking down of the classical hedonistic taxonomy; and the breakdown is typical of the best work done by the school. This move of the classifiers is, of course, nothing sudden; nor is it an accident. It means, in substance, only that the modern facts have increasingly shown themselves incompatible with the mechanical scheme of classical definitions, and that this discrepancy between the facts and the received categories has finally forced a breaking away from the old categories. The whole voluminous discussion of the capital concept, for the past twenty years or so, has, indeed, turned about this discrepancy between business practice and the hedonistic classification by means of which economists have tried to deal with this business practice. All expedients of classification, definition, refinement, and interpretation of technical phrases have been tried, except the surrender of the main position -- that economic conduct must be read in terms of the hedonistic calculus.(6*)

Under the stress of this controversy of interpretation, the hedonistic concept of capital as a congeries of "productive goods" has gradually and reluctantly, but hitherto not wholly, been replaced by something more serviceable. But this gain in serviceability has been won -- in so far as the achievement may be spoken of in the past tense -- at some cost to the hedonistic point of view. Such serviceability as the newly achieved interpretation of the capital concept has, it has because, and only so far as, it substitutes a pecuniary for a hedonistic construction of the phenomena of capitalisation. Among those who speak for the new (pecuniary) construction is Mr Fisher, although he is not by any means the freest of those who are breaking away. His position is, no doubt, deprecated by many taxonomic economists as being an irreverently, brutally iconoclastic innovation, quite indefensible on taxonomic grounds; but, after all, as Mr Fetter has shown in more courteous words,(7\*) it is an equivocal, or perhaps rather an irresolute position at the best.

"Capital", in the classical definition, was, as required by the hedonistic point of view, a congeries of what has latterly been named "productive goods." From such a concept of capital, which is hopelessly and increasingly out of touch with business usage, the theorists have been straining away; and Mr Fisher has borne a large part in the speculations that are leading up to the emancipation of theorists from the chore work required by that white elephant. But he is not content formally to give up the heirloom; although, as Mr Fetter indicates, he now makes little use of it except for parade. He offers two correlate definitions of capital: "capital wealth", i.e., productive goods, and "capital value", i.e., pecuniary capital.(8\*) The former of these, the authentic hedonistic concept, shortly drops out of the discussion, although it does not drop out so tracelessly as Mr Fetter's criticism may suggest. The argument then proceeds, almost throughout, on the concept of "capital value".(9\*) But there is a recurrent, and, one is tempted to say, dutiful, reminder that this "capital value", or capitalisation of values, is to be taken as the value of a congeries of tangible objects (productive goods); whereby a degree of taxonomic consistency with the authentic past and with the hedonistic postulate is formally maintained, and whereby also, dutifully and authentically, intangible assets are excluded from the capital concept, as already indicated above. Capital value is "simply the present worth of the future income from the specified capital."(10*) (p. 202); but this capital value, it is held, is always the value of tangible items (including persons?).

It is the uncanny office of the critic to deal impersonally with his author's work as an historical phenomenon. Under cover of this license it may be pardonable to speak badly and broadly of the logic of this retention of the authentic postulate that physically productive goods (including persons) alone are to be included in the capitalisation out of which capital value emerges. And what is here said in this connection is not to be taken as a presumptuous make-believe of reproducing the sequence of ideas by which Mr Fisher has arrived to trace the logical sequence between the main hedonistic body of theory and the historical outcome of its development at this point.

In the classical-Austrian scheme of theory the center and circumference of economic life is the production of what a writer on ethics has called "pleasant feeling." Pleasant feeling is produced only by tangible, physical objects (including persons), acting somehow upon the sensory. The inflow of pleasant feeling is "income" -- "psychic income" net and positive. The purpose of capital is to serve this end -- the increase of pleasant feeling -- and things are capital, in the authentic hedonistic scheme, by as much as they serve this end. Capital, therefore, must be tangible, material goods, since only tangible goods will stimulate the human sensory pleasantly. Intangible assets, being not physical, do not impinge upon the sensory; therefore they are not capital. Since they unavoidably are thrown prominently on the screen in the show of modern life, they must, consistently with the hedondistic conception, be explained away by construing them in terms of some authentic category of tangible items.

There is a second line of approach to the same conclusion comprised in the logical scheme of hedonistic economics, more cogent on practical grounds than that sketched above and perhaps of equally convincing metaphysical force. The hedonistic (classical-Austrian) economics is a system of taxonomic science -- a science of normalities. Its office is the definition and classification of "normal" phenomena, or, perhaps better, phenomena as they occur in the normal case. And in this normal case, when and so far as the laws of nature work out their ends unvitated, nature does all things well. This is also according to the ancient and authentic canons of taxonomic science. In the hedonistically normal scheme of life wasteful, disserviceable, or futile acts have no place.(11*) The current competitive, capitalistic business scheme of life is normal, when rightly seen in the hedonistic light. There is not (normally) in it anything of a wasteful, disserviceable, or futile character. Whatever phenomena do not fit into the scheme of normal economic life, as tested by the hedonistic postulate, are to be taken account of by way of exception. If there are discrepancies, in the way of waste, disserviceability, or futility, e.g., they are not inherent in the normal scheme and they do not call for incorporation in the theory of the situation in which they occur, except for interpretative elimination and correction. In this course the hedonistic economics, with its undoubting faith that whatever (normally) is is right, simply follows the rule of all authentic taxonomic science.

As indicated above, the normal end of capital, as of all the multifarious phenomena of economic life, is the production of pleasure and the prevention of pain; and in the Benthamite system of theory -- which includes the classical-Austrian economics -- the normal end of the life of man in society, economic and otherwise, is the greatest happiness of the greatest number. Such may not be the outcome in any given actual situation, but in so far as such is not the outcome the situation departs from the normal; and such departures from the normal do not properly concern the (hedonistic) "science" of economics, but fall authentically to the care of the "art" of economics, whose concern it is to find correctives for these, essentially sporadic, aberrations. Under the rule of normal serviceability nothing can be included in the theoretically right "capital summation" which does not go to swell the aggregate of hedonistic "services" to man --

nothing which is not "productive", in the sense of increasing the well-being of mankind at large. Persons may, indeed they "normally" should always, be productive in this sense, and persons, therefore, should properly be included in the capital summation.(12*)

In this normalised scheme of economic life all claims represented by negotiable instruments, e.g., must be led back, as is done by Mr Fisher,(13*) to tangible items of serviceable goods; and in its application to the concrete case, the actual situation, if follows from this rule that all such instruments are, normally, evidences of the ownership of such tangible items as serve the material needs of mankind at large. It follows also that there are, normally, no items of differential serviceability included among the property rights covered by negotiable instruments; that in the hedonistic theory of business there are no differential advantages and no differential or competitive gains; that the gain of each business man is, at the most, simply the sum of his own contributions to the aggregate of services that maintain the life and happiness of the community. This optimistic light shed on the business situation by the hedonistic postulate is one of the most valued, and for the wise quietist assuredly the most valuable, of the theoretical results following from the hedonistic taxonomy. And this optimistic light will fail with the surrender of the authentic position that capital is a congeries of physically productive goods. But while this light lasts the hedonistic economist is able to say that, although the scheme of economic life contemplated by him as normal is a competitive system, yet the gains of the competitors are in no degree of a competitive character; no one (normally) gains at the cost of another or at the cost of the community at large; nor does any one (normally) turn any part of his equipment of capital goods to use for a competitive or differential advantage. In this light, the competitive struggle is seen to work out as, in effect, a friendly rivalry in the service of mankind at large, with an eye single to the greatest happiness of the greatest number. If intangible assets are recongnised by the theory this comforting outlook on the business situation fails, because intangible assets are, in the main, of a differential effect only. Hence they are excluded by the logic of the hedonistic taxonomy.

Returning to a point left uncovered above (p. 120), it may be in place to look more narrowly into the definition of capital as 'capital value" arrived at by Mr Fisher, ably spoken for by Mr Fetter, and apparently in train to be accepted by many economists interested in questions of theory.(14*) On its face this formulation seems definite, tangible, and stable enough. Such a concept appears to serve the needs of business traffic. But it is a more delicate question, and more to the present purpose, whether the definition has the requisite stability and mechanical precision for the purposes of a taxonomy such as Mr Fisher's, which seeks to set up mutually exclusive categories of things distinguished from one another by statistically determined lines of demarcation. The question obtrudes itself, as regards this putative value of expected income: Whose imputation of value is to be accepted? Value, of course, is a fact of imputation; and it may seem a ready solution to say that the decision in this question of appraisement is rendered by a consensus of imputation between or among the parties concerned in the capitalisation. This consensus would be shown concretely by market quotations of securities, and it would be shown in generalised form by the familiar diagrams offered by all taxonomists of the marginal-utility school. But, concretely, there is not always a consensus of imputations as to the expected value of a given flow of income; in the case of unlisted securities, as well as of other capitalisable property in like case, the appeal to a consensus fails. And, in point of taxonomic theory, the marginal-utility curves apply to the case in hand only when and in so far as the property in question is the subject of a bargain; and, further, the diagrams of intersections and the like are of no avail for the cases, frequent enough in practice, where bargains are struck at the same time for different lots of the same line of goods at different heights on the ordinate. It is only by virtue of broad and untenable generalisations concerning the higgling of the market that the diagrams appear to cover a general proposition as to the actual value of property. The upshot of the matter is that a given block of capital need not, in practice it frequently does not, have one particular value at a given time; no more than a given expected flow of income need have one particular value alone imputed to it by all, or by a consensus of, the various parties in interest.

A summary review of an actual case taken from current business traffic may illustrate some of the difficulties of arriving, in detail, at such a definite and stable determination of capital value as will serve the needs of "capital summation" as expounded by Mr Fisher.

A relatively small and inconspicuous corporation managed by two men, A and B, had for a series of years been doing a successful, conservative business in one of the necessaries of life, and had achieved an enviable reputation for efficiency and reliability; that is to say, it had accumulated a large and valuable body of "good will." The only form of securities outstanding was common stock, unlisted, and held by relatively few stockholders. During the late winter and spring of the present year (1907), the managers of the company gathered from the course of the market that business in their line would probably slacken off appreciably in the immediate future, with small change of a prompt recovery. They determined to sell out and withdraw to another line of business, not similarly dependent on prices. To this end they set about buying in all the stock of their company, A-B, with a view to selling out the going concern to another corporation, C-D, whose appraisement of the future (imputation of value) was apparently more sanguine than their own. The outstanding shares of stock were bought in, during a period of some six weeks, by A and B bargaining separately with the several stockholders as opportunity offered, at prices ranging from about 105 to about 125. Meantime, negotiation had been going forward with company C-D for the sale of the concern as a whole on the basis of an inventory of the plant, including the stock of goods on hand. Both the plant and the stock of goods were somewhat extensive and scattered. With the inventory as a basis the concern was sold at an aggregate price which included a fair allowance for the intangible assets (good will) of the going concern. The inventory was taken on the basis of the last previous monthly price-current, and the transfer to C-D took place on that basis. As counted on by A-B, and as apparently not counted on by C-D, the next succeeding monthly price-current showed a decline in the market value of the stock of goods on hand of some nine or ten percent; and the subsequent course of the market, as well as of the volume of traffic in this line of business, has been of the same complexion. The transfer of the concern, all told, from A-B to C-D took place at figures which aggregated an advance of some 25 percent over the cost to A and B, counting the stock of the corporation at an average of the prices paid by them for such shares of stock as they bought in from other stockholders, which was rather more than one-half of all the outstanding stock.

The question now is: What, for purposes of "capital summation", should be taken as the basis of the capital value of corporation A-B last spring, say, at the date of the transfer to C-D, or at any date during the buying in of the outstanding stock? During all this time the "capital value" must have been something over 100 percent of the nominal capital, since none of the stock was bought at less than 105. But the shares of stocks were bought in, slatteringly, from 105 to 125, with an average in the neighborhood of 115; while the aggregate price of the going concern at the same time seems to have been in the neighborhood of 140 percent of the nominal capitalisation. Should the last transaction in the purchase of stock from day to day, running uncertainly between 105 and 125, be construed to revise the 'capital value" of the concern to that date? This would make the "capital value" skip capriciously back and forth within the 20 points of the margin, in attendance upon the last previous "consensus of imputation" between a given seller and one or the other of the two buyers. The final average of, say, 115, had not at that time been established, so that that figure could not be taken as a basis during the interval. Or should the stipulated price of the going concern rule the case, in the face of these transactions taking place at figures incompatible with it? Again, at the date of the transfer to C-D, was the "capital value" immediately before the transfer the (indefinite) rating given by the then owners, A and B; and was it, the next minute, to be counted at the price paid by C-D; or, at the nominal capitalisation; or, at the (indefinite) figure at which C-D might have been willing to sell? What further serves to muddle the whole question is the fact that the transfer price of the going concern had been agreed upon between A-B and C-D before the whole amount of the outstanding stock had been bought in by A-B.

This case, which is after all sufficiently commonplace, offers a chance for further refinements of confusion, but what has been said may serve to illustrate the point in question. The difficulty, it will be noticed, is a difficulty of classification, not of business procedure. There are no difficulties of mutual intelligibility among the various parties engaged in the transactions. The difficulties arise when it is attempted to define the phenomena for some (taxonomic) purpose not germane to the transactions in question, and to draw lines of demarcation that are of no effect in the business affairs in which these phenomena arise. The resulting confusion marks a taxonomic infirmity in the proposed capital concept, due to an endeavor to reach a definition from a metaphysical postulate (of hedonism) not comprised among the postulates on which business traffic proceeds.

This fable teaches that it is a wise hedonist who keeps his capital concept clear of all entanglement with 'capital value", and, more particularly, with the live business notion of capitalised earning-capacity.

## NOTES:

1. The Nature of Capital and Income, by Irving Fisher, New York, 1906.

2. Journal of Political Economy, March, 1907, "The Nature of Capital and Income". See also Mr Fisher's reply in the same journal, July, 1907, "Professor Fetter on Capital and Income."

3. See chapter ii, section 6, pp. 24031; also section 10.

4. Contrary to Mr Fisher's elaborate doctrine of property rights as defined by mechanical limits. -- Chapter ii.

5. Cf. Journal of Political Economy, papers cited above.

6. The argument will return to the hedonistic calculus presently to show how the logic of this calculus has forced the theory at certain points.

7. Journal of Political Economy, as above, pp. 143-144.

8. Pp. 66-67, 327, and elsewhere.

9. Mr Fetter, in advance of Mr Fisher in the position taken if not in priority of departure, advocates discarding the older (authentic hedonistic) concept, in form as well as in fact.

10. In this and similar passages Mr Fisher appears to be in search of a more competent phrase, which has been used, but which he apparently has not met with -- "putative

earning-capacity." Certain infirmities of such a definition, whether under one phrase or another, for the taxonomic purpose, will be indicated presently.

11. Cf., e.g., Clark, Essentials of Economic Theory, passim. -- "Each man who gets in a normal way, any income at all performs one or more productive functions" etc. - p. 92.

12. What is to be done, theoretically, with persons leading disserviceable or futile lives, "undesirable citizens", does not clearly appear. They are undesirable, but they are of the human breed and so are presumably to be included in the normal human aggregate whose "greatest number" are elected for the "greatest happiness" by the (normally) benevolent laws of nature. The suggestion is, of course, obvious that they should be deducted from the gross aggregate of items -- i.e., algebraically added in as negative magnitudes -- so as to leave a net algebraic sum of positively serviceable capital goods, including persons. The like might apparently be done with impersonal material items which are wastefully or noxiously employed.

But the converse suggestion is at least equally cogent, that such disserviceable items, personal and impersonal, are simply abnormal, aberrant, exceptional, and that therefore they simply drop tracelessly out of the theoretical scheme, so as to the theoretically correct "summation" as large as it would be had these disserviceable negative times items not been present. That is to say, the theoretically correct net aggregate serviceability is the same as the gross serviceability; since the negative quantities actually present among the aggregate of items are not normally present, and are, therefore, theoretically non-existent.

There is a third alternative. The abnormal disserviceable items being indubitably present in fact, and some part of them being present with the hedonistically sacred stamp of the human breed, it may be that, in the apprehension of the adepts, should this problem of taxonomy present itself to them, at least so much of the disserviceable productive goods as are human beings should be counted in; but, since they are persons, and since it is the normal estate of man to be serviceable to his fellows, they should be theoretically counted as normally serviceable, and therefore included in the net aggregate of serviceability at the magnitude of serviceability normally imputable to them. What rule should guide in fixing the true magnitude of imputed normal serviceability for such disserviceable persons in such a case is a further problem of taxonomy which would take the present argument too far afield. This much seems clear, however, that under this third alternative the net aggregate serviceability to be imputed to the sum of capital goods (including persons) should exceed the actual aggregate serviceability by the addition of an amount approximately equal to the disservice rendered by the disserviceable persons in question.

13. Chapter ii, especially sections 4-9, and pp. 93-96.

14. The value of capital is the discounted value of the expected income" (p. 328). "It is found by discounting (or 'capitalising') the value of the income expected from the wealth of property." (p. 330). "Capital today may be defined as economical wealth expressed in terms of the general unit of value." (Fetter, Principles of Economics, p. 115)... "every good becoming capital when it is capitalised, that is, when the totality of its uses is expressed as a present sum of values." (Ibid. p. 116) It has elsewhere been characterised as "capitalisation of putative earning capacity." The latter is perhaps the more serviceable definition, being nearer to the concept of capital current in the business community.

www.ingramcontent.com/pod-product-compliance
Lightning Source LLC
Chambersburg PA
CBHW030241180626
46810CB00008B/3236